Portfoolio 25

· THE YEAR'S BEST CANADIAN EDITORIAL CARTOONS ·

MAJORITY...

AISLIN '11
MONTREAL
THE GAZETTE

EDITED WITH TEXT BY WARREN CLEMENTS

McArthur & Company
Toronto

First published in Canada in 2011 by
McArthur & Company
67 Mowat Ave., Suite 241
Toronto, Ontario
M6K 3E3
www.mcarthur-co.com

www.canadiancartoonists.com

ISBN: 978-1-55278-991-9

Edited by: Warren Clements
Text by: Warren Clements
Design by: Kendra Martin

 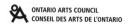

Canada Council   Conseil des Arts
for the Arts   du Canada

ONTARIO ARTS COUNCIL
CONSEIL DES ARTS DE L'ONTARIO

The publisher would like to acknowledge the financial support of the
Government of Canada through the Canada Book Fund and the
Canada Council for our publishing activities. The publisher further wishes
to acknowledge the financial support of the Ontario Arts Council and
the OMDC for our publishing program.

Printed and bound in Canada by Transcontinental

10 9 8 7 6 5 4 3 2 1

BRIAN GABLE, *The Globe and Mail*

DE ADDER, *Metro*

INTRODUCTION

Editorial cartoonists lead a roller-coaster life. One day they're joking about a world fixated on Oprah, and the next they're grappling with the tragedy of Japan's earthquake and tsunami, or marvelling at the use of Twitter in the Arab Spring. Canada gave them a jolt this year by handing Stephen Harper's Conservatives a majority, making the NDP the Official Opposition, bumping the Liberals to third place and kicking the Bloc around the block. You have to be ready for anything in this business.

Like actors in a long-running soap opera, the cast keeps changing. Revisit the decline and fall of Michael Ignatieff, whose chief political failing wasn't that he didn't come back for you but that he didn't have a comeback for you-know-who. Say adieu to Gilles Duceppe. Watch British Columbia's Gordon Campbell stub his toe on the HST (the pronunciation of which is close to an expletive in French). It's always sad for cartoonists to lose such dependable material; Geoff Olson even drew a cartoon (included here) about his reliance on Campbell to inspire his next day's work.

The upside is that new figures arrive to provide grist for the cartoonist's mill. Kim Jong-il begat Kim Jong-un. Will and Kate – sorry, the Duke and Duchess of Cambridge – became an official couple rather than a couple-in-waiting. Toronto said hello to a new mayor, Rob Ford, whose galvanizing effect on downtown Torontonians was deftly captured in Brian Gable's NNA-winning cartoon on page three. Julian Assange arrived with WikiLeaks, the fuss that launched a thousand diplomatic slips.

As ever, many thanks to the cartoonists and their newspapers for making this material available. Eight tiny caricatures sit atop the title on the front cover. All are borrowed from cartoons within this book, so put aside *Where's Waldo* and play a game of Where's Liz May – much the same game played by viewers of this year's federal leaders' debate. Happy perusing.

BADO, *Le Droit*, Ottawa

Against the advice of pretty much everyone, Stephen Harper's Conservative government started the summer of 2010 by eliminating the mandatory long-form census that Statistics Canada had long used to gather complex data to assist in decision-making. The head of Statscan quit in protest. The Office of the Privacy Commissioner said it had received only three complaints about the census in the past decade. Industry Minister Tony Clement said the concerns of the business community and others were "overwrought."

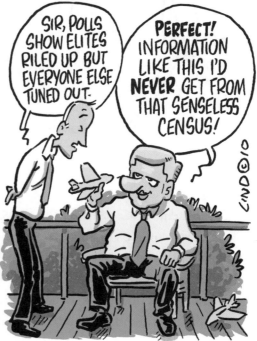

LIND, *This Bright Future*

RICE

Liberals and New Democrats attacked the Conservatives for ordering sixty-five F-35 fighter jets for $16-billion ($9-billion plus maintenance) without seeking competitive tenders. Liberal Leader Michael Ignatieff, criticized for being aloof and having no clear positions, would spend the summer attending barbecues across the country to paint himself as a smart, regular guy. In August, the ship *MV Sun Sea* arrived off the west coast of British Columbia carrying more than four hundred and fifty Tamil migrants, all of whom promptly claimed refugee status.

TYRELL

Michael Ignatieff's summer tour draws to a close
(July 14, July 26, August 17, September 1)
"There. I've done it!"

CHAPLEAU, *La Presse*, Montreal

CORRIGAN, *Toronto Star*

DEWAR, QMI Agency

PASCAL, *The Gazette*, Montreal

PERRY

(The United States leaves Iraq.) "Here, kid. It's all yours now."

GARNOTTE, *Le Devoir*, Montreal

After invading Iraq and staying for seven years, the United States began a formal withdrawal of troops scheduled to be completed by the end of 2011. In September, economists predicted that the longest U.S. recession since the Second World War would be followed by one of the slowest economic recoveries. The rest of the world had its own troubles. BP permanently sealed its blown-out Macondo well in the Gulf of Mexico, almost half a year after an explosion on the Deepwater Horizon drilling platform caused the worst oil spill in history. Ontario Superior Court judge Susan Himel struck down three central provisions of Canada's anti-prostitution laws, ruling them unconstitutional. The laws remained in force pending an appeal in 2011.

"In medicine, they speak of a vegetative coma."

CÔTÉ, *Le Soleil*, Quebec City

DONATO, *Toronto Sun*

LARTER, *Calgary Herald*

CUMMINGS, *Winnipeg Free Press*

MURPHY, *The Province*, Vancouver

CLEMENT, *National Post*

STREET, *Fisher*

DONATO, *Toronto Sun*

MacKINNON, *The Chronicle Herald*, Halifax

British Columbia Liberal Premier Gordon Campbell, whose introduction of a harmonized sales tax after he won re-election in 2009 prompted a successful petition against the tax, said he and Finance Minister Colin Hansen would retreat on the HST if it was defeated in a referendum late in 2011. After NDP Leader Jack Layton leaned on his rural MPs to support the long-gun registry, which was intended to let police know who owned hunting rifles and shotguns, the opposition majority in the House of Commons defeated Conservative efforts to dismantle the system. Canada's police chiefs supported the registry. The Conservatives pledged to end it if given a majority.

RAESIDE, *Times Colonist*, Victoria

MURPHY, *The Province*, Vancouver

PARKINS, *The Globe and Mail*

OLSON, *Vancouver Courier*

GABLE, *The Globe and Mail*

MURPHY, *The Province*, Vancouver

The NDP would save the registry...

FLEG, *Yahoo Quebec*

In October, after being trapped for sixty-nine days nearly half a mile underground, thirty-three miners in Chile were rescued in an ambitious operation that held the world spellbound. French President Nicolas Sarkozy's proposed pension reforms were met with violent protests. In a fiscal update, federal Finance Minister Jim Flaherty predicted that Canada would start running a budget surplus by 2016. Parliamentary Budget Officer Kevin Page said there was an eighty-five-per-cent chance Flaherty would miss his targets.

DEWAR, QMI Agency

HARROP, *The Vancouver Sun*

CHAPLEAU, *La Presse*, Montreal

Surprise! A 34th returns to the surface.

"I assure you, I'm a Chilean miner!"

GABLE, *The Globe and Mail*

"I'm the one who decides when we retreat – understood?"

GARNOTTE, *Le Devoir*, Montreal

RICE

MOU, *Toronto Star*

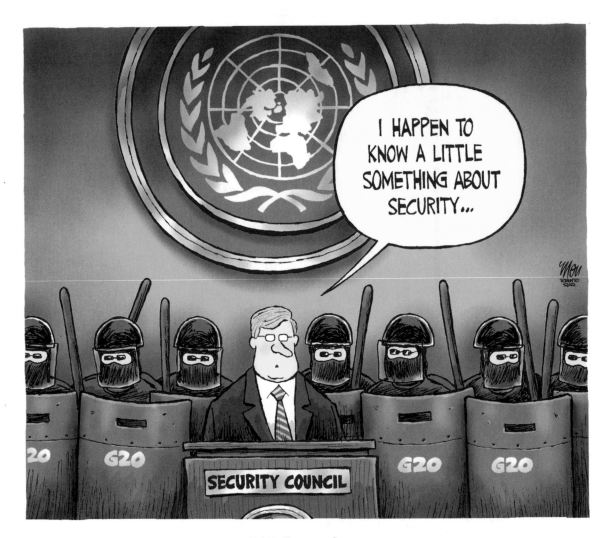

MOU, *Toronto Star*

Despite a concerted effort by Stephen Harper and Foreign Minister Lawrence Cannon to secure a two-year seat on the United Nations Security Council, Canada was passed over in favour of Portugal. Omar Khadr, a Canadian who had been captured in Afghanistan in 2002 at age fifteen and accused of killing a U.S. medic, remained in the U.S. prison at Guantanamo Bay, with the Harper government doing little to assist him. On October 25, he pleaded guilty to murder, terrorism and spying as part of a plea bargain that would allow him, after another year, to return to Canada to serve the remainder of his sentence. The U.S. midterm elections on November 2 saw control of the House of Representatives pass to the Republicans, many of them members of the ultra-right Tea Party movement.

MACKAY, *The Hamilton Spectator*

LARTER, *Calgary Herald*

MacKINNON, *The Chronicle Herald*, Halifax

UN Security Council.
Mr. Cannon's retreat.

"We didn't lose. We withdrew just in time."

GARNOTTE, *Le Devoir*, Montreal

HARROP, *The Vancouver Sun*

JENKINS, *The Globe and Mail*

DEWAR, QMI Agency

MACKAY, *The Hamilton Spectator*

AISLIN, *The Gazette*, Montreal

MacKINNON, *The Chronicle Herald*, Halifax

ROSEN, *The Montreal Mirror*

MAYES, *Edmonton Journal*

The federal government, which had said critics were overreacting to a takeover bid for Saskatchewan-based Potash Corp. by Australian mining giant BHP Billiton, eventually blocked the bid after lobbying by Saskatchewan and other provinces. B.C. Premier Gordon Campbell, massively unpopular because of the HST, said he would resign after seventeen years as Liberal leader and nearly ten as premier. Carole James, leader of the B.C. NDP, had her own troubles with a brewing caucus revolt. Danny Williams, the popular premier of Newfoundland, announced that he too would step down.

AISLIN, *The Gazette*, Montreal

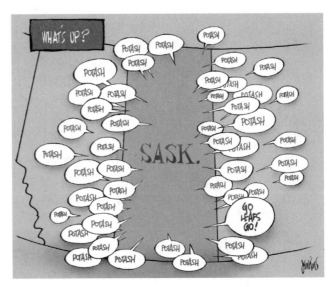

JENKINS, *The Globe and Mail*

JENKINS, *The Globe and Mail*

JENKINS, *The Globe and Mail*

ARNOULD, *The Georgia Straight*

ARNOULD, *The Georgia Straight*

MURPHY, *The Province*, Vancouver

PARKINS, *The Globe and Mail*

RAESIDE, *Times Colonist*, Victoria

DEWAR, QMI Agency

Conservative senators, a majority in the Senate thanks to Stephen Harper's assiduous stacking of the appointed House, defeated a bill on climate change that had been passed by the Commons. North Korea marked the news that Kim Jong-un would succeed his father Kim Jong-il as dictator by unveiling a uranium-enrichment facility and shelling an inhabited South Korean island. Former U.S. president George W. Bush released his memoirs. In November, after a California airport security guard conducted a groin check of a passenger and the man snapped, "Don't touch my junk," a video clip of the moment became an Internet hit.

MACKAY, *The Hamilton Spectator*

BADO, *Le Droit*, Ottawa

DEWAR, QMI Agency

CLEMENT, *National Post*

CÔTÉ, *Le Soleil*, Quebec City

BUSH PUBLIE SES MÉMOIRES

J'AI HÂTE DE LIRE ÇA!

CHAPLEAU, *La Presse*, Montreal

Bush publishes his memoirs.
"I can't wait to read them."

WAR AND PEAS AND WMDs

MY MEMOIRS

BY W.

ROSEN, *The Montreal Mirror*

MacKINNON, *The Chronicle Herald*, Halifax

AISLIN, *The Gazette*, Montreal

CORRIGAN, *Toronto Star*

Rumours circulated that federal Defence Minister Peter MacKay would resign because he had been ignored or overruled by Stephen Harper on two major issues: whether to keep a Canadian military presence in Afghanistan until 2014 instead of 2011 and whether to let the United Arab Emirates, where Canada had a strategic airbase, have prime landing spots in Canada for the national airline. MacKay said he would stay on as minister. U.S. President Barack Obama lashed out at Julian Assange and his WikiLeaks website, which was releasing hundreds of thousands of pilfered letters from U.S. diplomats as well as U.S. Defence Department documents discussing the wars in Afghanistan and Iraq.

GABLE, *The Globe and Mail*

DOLIGHAN, QMI Agency

43

JENKINS, *The Globe and Mail*

ROSEN, *The Montreal Mirror*

PERRY

PASCAL, *The Gazette*, Montreal

DUSAN, *Toronto Star*

BADO, *Le Droit*, Ottawa

CÔTÉ, *Le Soleil*, Quebec City

"What's WikiLeaks?"
"It's like grandma and my aunt, but electronic."

In the series "Two Hands on the Wheel": The Untouchables.
(Licence plate: Quebec Liberal Party; sign at back: A commission of inquiry, please.)

GARNOTTE, *Le Devoir*, Montreal

Quebec Premier Jean Charest, whose 2008 election slogan was "two hands on the wheel" (in search of a majority, which he received), promised to create an anti-corruption unit in Quebec modelled on New York City's Department of Investigations. He continued to dismiss calls for a full public inquiry into allegations of corruption in the construction industry and links to the awarding of government contracts. (Public pressure would eventually force him to call such an inquiry in October 2011.) A new ethics code adopted by the National Assembly required Charest to forfeit a supplemental salary his party had been giving him.

In December, Rob Ford was elected mayor of Toronto on a promise to slash public spending and stop the "gravy train." He invited hockey commentator and self-described pit bull Don Cherry to introduce him at his first council meeting. Cherry talked about "all the pinkos out there that ride bicycles."

He gives up his Quebec Liberal Party salary!
He dreams of a simpler life!
Sharek Forever After: The Final Chapter.

CHAPLEAU, *La Presse*, Montreal

"Ah, violinist. What a fine profession."

GARNOTTE, *Le Devoir*, Montreal

AISLIN, *The Gazette*, Montreal

TYRELL, *The Hamilton Spectator*

DONATO, *Toronto Sun*

KRIEGER, *The Province*, Vancouver

RAESIDE, *Times Colonist*, Victoria

B.C. NDP Leader Carole James, unable to appease dissidents in her caucus, said she would step down. A climate-change conference in Cancun ended with only vague talk of extending the 1997 Kyoto Protocol to reduce greenhouse gases. Canada said it would not commit itself to a new series of Kyoto obligations. Stephen Harper capped off the year by playing and singing the John Lennon song "Imagine" with an impromptu band at a Conservative get-together.

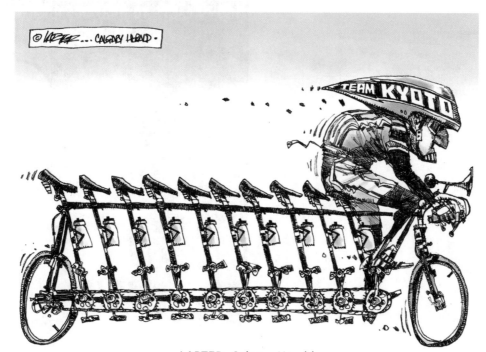

LARTER, *Calgary Herald*

MAYES, *Edmonton Journal*

MOU, *Toronto Star*

MACKAY, *The Hamilton Spectator*

OLSON, *Vancouver Courier*

LARTER, *Calgary Herald*

As 2011 began, Canadians remained in thrall to new media and technology. Pittsburgh Penguins star Sidney Crosby was sidelined after blows received in games on January 1 and 5, making him the latest National Hockey League player to suffer concussions on the job. Montreal Canadiens winger Max Pacioretty would be similarly hurt in March. NHL commissioner Gary Bettman responded that one was bound to see concussions in a physical game.

INTERNET

DUSAN, *Toronto Star*

AISLIN, *The Gazette*, Montreal

"It must be terrible to live in obscurity."

CÔTÉ, *Le Soleil*, Quebec City

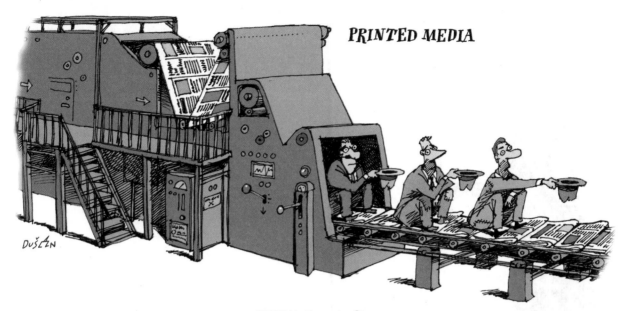

PRINTED MEDIA

DUSAN, *Toronto Star*

SOCIAL MEDIA

MacKINNON, *The Chronicle Herald*, Halifax

KRIEGER, *The Province*, Vancouver

KRIEGER, *The Province*, Vancouver

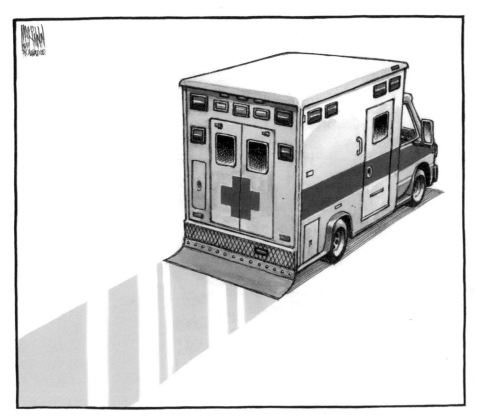

MacKINNON, *The Chronicle Herald*, Halifax

GABLE, *The Globe and Mail*

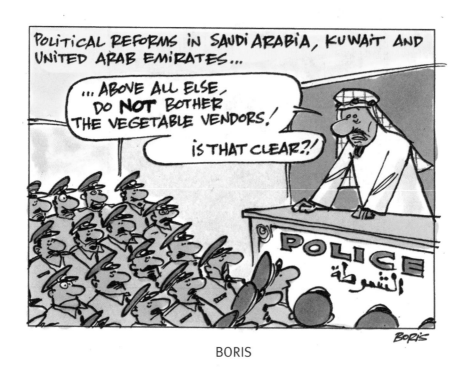

BORIS

Protests erupted in Tunisia after a street vendor set fire to himself because a police officer had confiscated his vegetable cart. President Zine El Abidine Ben Ali surrendered power. As demonstrations followed in other countries – Bahrain, Egypt, Yemen, Libya, Syria – the surge to overthrow dictators was dubbed the Arab Spring, fuelled by Twitter and other social media. Most of the dictators remained in place. Egyptian protesters took to the streets after photos of a businessman beaten to death by police were posted on the Net. President Hosni Mubarak would hand over power in February.

MAYES, *Edmonton Journal*

NEMO

CÔTÉ, *Le Soleil*, Quebec City

DEWAR, QMI Agency

DOLIGHAN, QMI Agency

McCULLOUGH

THE SOCIAL NETWORK

DE ADDER, *Metro*

CLEMENT, *National Post*

DONATO, *Toronto Sun*

HARROP, *The Vancouver Sun*

CÔTÉ, *Le Soleil*, Quebec City

BORIS

CUMMINGS, *Winnipeg Free Press*

DEWAR, QMI Agency

MOU, *Toronto Star*

Federal Environment Minister Peter Kent defended Alberta's oil sands as "ethical" because Canada wasn't a dictatorship – a point borrowed from commentator Ezra Levant. Motorists were coping with rising prices at gas stations.

LIND, *Footprint in Mouth*

68

PARKINS/SHERMAN, *The Walrus*

RICE

The price of gas...

FLEG, *Yahoo Quebec*

PERRY

PRICE

DUSAN, *Toronto Star*

JENKINS, *The Globe and Mail*

In January, Stephen Harper marked his fifth anniversary as prime minister. The air was electric with speculation about whether the opposition parties would force an election. The Liberals were faring poorly in the polls. Harper hoped his Conservatives would make a breakthrough in previously Tory-averse Toronto.

ROSEN, *The Montreal Mirror*

MAYES, *Edmonton Journal*

CHAPLEAU, *La Presse*, Montreal

McCULLOUGH

MOU, *Toronto Star*

GABLE, *The Globe and Mail*

CORRIGAN, *Toronto Star*

AISLIN, *The Gazette*, Montreal

Confronted with protests against his regime, Libyan dictator Moammar Gadhafi reacted so brutally that, after a much-criticized delay, the United Nations Security Council ordered the establishment of a no-fly zone over the country. NATO began to bomb the country. Civilians were killed. Canada participated in the operation, which was called Odyssey Dawn. Months later, Gadhafi was still in power, and it was unclear who exactly would replace him. (He would be caught and summarily killed by his captors in October.)

SEBASTIAN

MacKINNON, *The Chronicle Herald*, Halifax

I'M MORE RESOLUTE THAN YOUR RESOLUTIONS!

BADO, *Le Droit*, Ottawa

Harper imposes severe sanctions on Libya.

"Okay, okay. I give up."

HARPER IMPOSE DES SANCTIONS SÉVÈRES À LA LIBYE

OK D'ABORD, JE ME RENDS!

CHAPLEAU, *La Presse*, Montreal

McCULLOUGH

RAESIDE, *Times Colonist*, Victoria

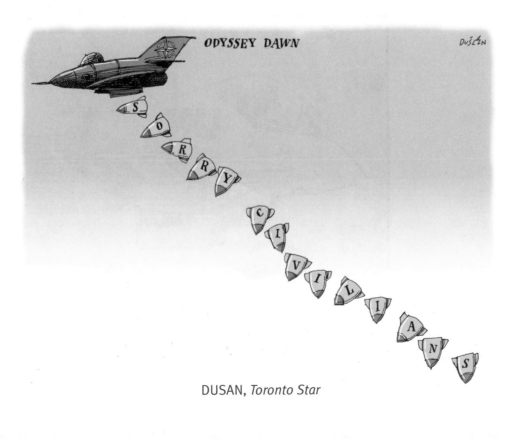

DUSAN, *Toronto Star*

NATO THOUGHT PROCESS

MURPHY, *The Province*, Vancouver

"TAKE THAT, GADHAFI!!"

MAYES, *Edmonton Journal*

BORIS

CUMMINGS, *Winnipeg Free Press*

PERRY

MURPHY, *The Province*, Vancouver

The B.C. Liberals elected Christy Clark as their new leader, automatically making her the new premier. She took steps to save the HST. (To no avail; the public would reject it in an August referendum.) The largest recorded earthquake in Japan's history struck that country's northeastern coast, followed by a 10-metre tsunami. Twenty-five thousand people were listed as dead or missing. Beyond the heartbreak of that tragedy, there were fears of widespread contamination from nuclear reactors damaged by the disaster.

PARKINS, *The Globe and Mail*

RAESIDE, *Times Colonist*, Victoria

MACKAY, *The Hamilton Spectator*

NEMO

85

GARNOTTE, *Le Devoir*, Montreal

GRASTON, *Windsor Star*

BADO, *Le Droit*, Ottawa

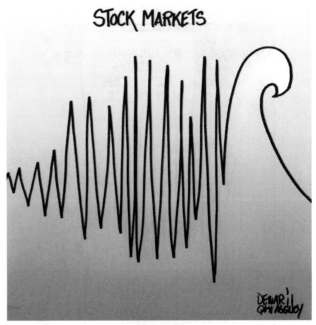

STOCK MARKETS

DEWAR, QMI Agency

CUMMINGS, *Winnipeg Free Press*

PERRY

The Canadian Press said a government directive had been sent to public servants in late 2010 instructing them to refer to the "Harper government" rather than the "Government of Canada." Spurred by public protests, the Quebec government said it would take action on fracking, the extraction of natural gas from shale rock by hydraulic fracturing. Exploration would be put on hold for thirty months pending an environmental study, but some fracking would continue for "scientific" purposes. The shale-gas lobby's chief spokesman, André Caillé, had had a rough time of it and was replaced by former Quebec premier Lucien Bouchard. A report from Parliamentary Budget Officer Kevin Page said buying sixty-five F-35 fighter-bombers would cost seventy per cent more than the government had estimated.

MacKINNON, *The Chronicle Herald*, Halifax

MURPHY, *The Province*, Vancouver

"Hmm, if only we could harness all that energy…"

(Placards: No to shale gas. Green energy. Not in my backyard.)

BORIS

André Caillé's burnout.

"Shale gas….
Shale gas…
You could have warned me the stuff was flammable."

CHAPLEAU, *La Presse*, Montreal

LARTER, *Calgary Herald*

CÔTÉ, *Le Soleil*, Quebec City

JENKINS, *The Globe and Mail*

In March, Peter Milliken, Speaker of the House of Commons, said the government was very likely in contempt of Parliament on two scores. First, it had failed to provide proper estimates for the cost of its proposed tough-on-crime legislation, which would see the building of more prisons. Second, International Co-operation Minister Bev Oda had misled Parliament in her statements about a 2009 decision to cut funding to the aid group Kairos. The document that denied the funding was altered with the insertion of a "not," so that senior civil servants appeared to be endorsing the refusal when in fact they had proposed that Kairos be funded. Talk of forcing an election continued.

MAYES, *Edmonton Journal*

DOLIGHAN, QMI Agency

ONLY THE LONELY...

CORRIGAN, *Toronto Star*

MURPHY, *The Province*, Vancouver

MOU, *Toronto Star*

MURPHY, *The Province*, Vancouver

GARNOTTE, *Le Devoir*, Montreal

Last wishes of
the condemned:
(Budget. Ethics.)
"Which would you
prefer?"

GRASTON, *Windsor Star*

MOU, *Toronto Star*

BORIS

PASCAL, *The Gazette*, Montreal

CHAPLEAU, *La Presse*, Montreal

Ignatieff takes possession of his campaign bus. "You don't think it's missing a little something eye-catching on the side of my bus, like for instance a photo of m–" "NO!"

DE ADDER, Metro

Finance Minister Jim Flaherty tabled his budget. None of the opposition parties supported it. Days later, in a vote of no-confidence, the House of Commons found the government in contempt of Parliament. An election was called for May 2. Stephen Harper warned voters that if they didn't give his Conservatives a majority, the Liberals, NDP and Bloc Québécois would form a coalition and the world would end, or something like that. Conservative attack ads against Liberal Leader Michael Ignatieff, who had lived abroad for many years, said: "He didn't come back for you." The Liberals responded with their own attack ads. Ignatieff dragged his feet before finally vowing he would not form a coalition. NDP Leader Jack Layton was criticized for making unaffordable promises. Stephen Harper played and sang "Imagine" with a Winnipeg girl famous on the Internet as a Lady Gaga fan. The video of the duet was posted on YouTube, but was removed by order of Yoko Ono. U.S. businessman Donald Trump, saying he might run to be U.S. president, sided with the birthers, conspiracy theorists who refused to believe Barack Obama was born in the United States (he was, in Hawaii) unless they saw his long-form birth certificate.

PERRY

CLEMENT, *National Post*

PASCAL, *The Gazette*, Montreal

MAYES, *Edmonton Journal*

RAESIDE, *Times Colonist*, Victoria

OLSON, *Vancouver Courier*

PERRY

GRASTON, *Windsor Star*

MACKAY, *The Hamilton Spectator*

"The Haitians elected a singer who thinks he's a politician."

"And we elected a politician who thinks he's a singer."

GARNOTTE, *Le Devoir*, Montreal

RAESIDE, *Times Colonist*, Victoria

TYRELL, *The Hamilton Spectator*

McCULLOUGH

OLSON, *Vancouver Courier*

AISLIN, *The Gazette*, Montreal

McCULLOUGH

TYRELL, *The Hamilton Spectator*

Stephen Harper, Michael Ignatieff, Jack Layton and Gilles Duceppe squared off in a televised debate. The broadcasters barred Green Party Leader Elizabeth May from participating because her party had no seats in the House of Commons. The NDP gained traction in Quebec at the expense of Bloc Québécois Leader Gilles Duceppe, in part by promising to reopen the Constitution to secure Quebec's approval. The Sun News Network took to the air as a right-wing cable news/opinion channel.

CLEMENT, *National Post*

ROSEN, *The Montreal Mirror*

DOLIGHAN, QMI Agency

DONATO, *Toronto Sun*

McCULLOUGH

LARTER, *Calgary Herald*

MOU, *Toronto Star*

Finally the four leaders are in agreement!
"What a ridiculous set design."
"It's truly ugly."
"We're stuck in a shipping container?"
"I hope it won't be the same for the French debate."

CHAPLEAU, *La Presse*, Montreal

GABLE, *The Globe and Mail*

PASCAL, *The Gazette*, Montreal

"If a vote for Layton is a vote for Harper, and a vote for the Bloc is a vote for Harper, and a vote for Ignatieff is a vote for Harper... why do they have elections?"

CÔTÉ, *Le Soleil*, Quebec City

"He can't hold on till May 2."

CÔTÉ, *Le Soleil*, Quebec City

DONATO, *Toronto Sun*

MURPHY, *The Province*, Vancouver

PARKINS, *Times Educational Supplement*

The April 29 wedding of Prince William and Catherine Middleton (the Duke and Duchess of Cambridge) was notable for the buzz about who was invited (hello, singer Elton John), the speculation over what dress Kate would wear and the fuss over who was wearing what fascinator, a sort of forward-placed hat.

117

DEWAR, QMI Agency

Predictions on that Royal Wedding Frock

Will not attempt to outdo Diana's in ruffles and bows

Dress won't be so voluminous as to encourage squatters

Retro bustle will not be so big that Banksy can't help himself

Train won't be long enough to allow folks in Scotland to hitch rides on it

And to show some empathy for the financially afflicted, the tiara will be a rental

MURPHY, *The Province*, Vancouver

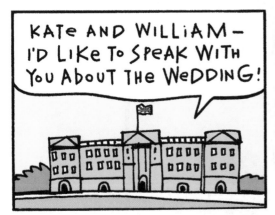

KATE AND WILLIAM— I'D LIKE TO SPEAK WITH YOU ABOUT THE WEDDING!

I'VE HAD A CALL FROM STEPHEN HARPER — HE WANTS TO PLAY PIANO DURING THE CEREMONY.

MICHAEL IGNATIEFF ALSO CALLED! HE WANTS TO SING TENOR AND DISCUSS KANT.

DON CHERRY WOULD LIKE TO DONATE A COUPLE OF SUITS FOR YOU AND PHILIP!

AND HOWIE MANDEL WANTS TO PROVIDE ENTERTAINMENT— SOMETHING ABOUT A RUBBER GLOVE ON HIS HEAD!

THERE'S ONLY ONE THING TO DO!

IN OTHER NEWS, BRITAIN TODAY SEVERED ALL RELATIONS WITH CANADA.

HARROP, *The Vancouver Sun*

RICE

STREET, *Fisher*

In the May 2 federal election, Stephen Harper's Conservatives won a majority. Jack Layton's New Democrats, thanks to a surge in Quebec, formed the Official Opposition with a remarkably young crop of new MPs. Michael Ignatieff's Liberals were reduced to a third party. Gilles Duceppe's Bloc Québécois was all but wiped out. Both Ignatieff and Duceppe would soon announce their resignations. Bob Rae was chosen as acting leader of the Liberal Party.

TYRELL

GABLE, *The Globe and Mail*

RICE

"Relax, unwind a little. I'm here for a while and I'm using a long fuse"

SEBASTIAN

LIND, *Footprint in Mouth*

"Fifty-nine Quebec MPs. I have fifty-nine Quebec MPs in Ottawa!"

CÔTÉ, *Le Soleil*, Quebec City

GABLE, *The Globe and Mail*

ARNOULD, *The Georgia Straight*

BADO, *Le Droit*, Ottawa

DE ADDER, *Metro*

LARTER, *Calgary Herald*

MURPHY, *The Province*, Vancouver

MOU, *Toronto Star*

RAE TAKES THE HELM...

LARTER, *Calgary Herald*

CUMMINGS, *Winnipeg Free Press*

GABLE, *The Globe and Mail*

OLSON

In May, U.S. Navy Seals shot and killed al-Qaeda leader Osama bin Laden in a walled compound in Pakistan. Questions were raised about how much the Pakistani government knew about bin Laden's presence there. The United States said it buried bin Laden at sea and had photographs of the body, but would not release them for reasons of taste and for fear al-Qaeda would use them to stir up anger.

PASCAL, *The Gazette*, Montreal

CLEMENT, *National Post*

PERRY

AISLIN, *The Gazette*, Montreal

CLEMENT, *National Post*

Dominique Strauss-Kahn, head of the International Monetary Fund, was arrested in New York for an alleged sexual assault against a maid in his hotel room, a charge he denied and which would be later dropped. He was replaced as IMF head. Since he had been a leading presidential contender in France, his arrest was seen as a lucky break for his opponent, French President Nicolas Sarkozy. Sheila Fraser, scourge of overspending, retired in May as Canada's auditor-general. Her final report criticized the funding of $50-million worth of projects in federal minister Tony Clement's riding without paper records or input from civil servants, before the 2010 G8 and G20 conferences in Ontario. The money, under the control of John Baird (infrastructure minister at the time), came from an $83-million fund approved by Parliament to relieve congestion at border crossings. Clement's riding of Parry Sound-Muskoka was three hundred kilometres from the border.

BADO, *Le Droit*, Ottawa

FLEG, *Le Soleil*

MacKINNON, *The Chronicle Herald*, Halifax

CORRIGAN, *Toronto Star*

DOLIGHAN, QMI Agency

MacKINNON, *The Chronicle Herald*, Halifax

HARROP, *The Vancouver Sun*

PERRY

Canada's best and brightest...

McCULLOUGH

On the Senate floor, a page created a furor by holding up a handmade stop sign saying "Stop Harper" as Governor-General David Johnston prepared to read the Speech from the Throne. She was fired. Greece, which had been bailed out before by Germany and the wealthier nations in the European Union, would be bailed out again for the sake of the euro zone. Other EU members had their own financial troubles.

BADO, *Le Droit*, Ottawa

ROSEN, *The Montreal Mirror*

DUSAN, *Toronto Star*

GABLE, *The Globe and Mail*

DONATO, *Toronto Sun*

Conservative Finance Minister Jim Flaherty delivered the federal budget, essentially the same one he had presented in March. It called for massive spending cuts to reduce the deficit. One new element was a pledge to eliminate direct subsidies for political parties, phasing out the $2-a-vote subsidy introduced by then-prime-minister Jean Chrétien in 2003.

MACKAY, *The Hamilton Spectator*

LARTER, *Calgary Herald*

MAYES, *Edmonton Journal*

On June 15, after the Boston Bruins defeated the Vancouver Canucks in the deciding game of the Stanley Cup finals in Vancouver, the worst riot in the city's modern history broke out. Participants photographed themselves while vandalizing cars and shops, and posted the photos online. After the riot, people horrified by the event went online to track down and expose those caught on camera.

KRIEGER, *The Province*, Vancouver

MacKINNON, *The Chronicle Herald*, Halifax

MURPHY, *The Province*, Vancouver

DOLIGHAN, QMI Agency

DEWAR, QMI Agency

McCULLOUGH

MAYES, *Edmonton Journal*

After postal workers staged a series of rotating strikes, Canada Post locked out forty-eight thousand employees. Within two weeks, Parliament passed special legislation ordering them back to work. After buying the Atlanta Thrashers and moving them north to Winnipeg, Mark Chipman and True North Sports & Entertainment Ltd. made it official that the NHL team's new name would be a familiar old one: the Jets. In July, newlyweds William and Kate visited Canada. Stops included the Calgary Stampede. As news spread that phone hacking by British newspaper News of the World had included the erasing of messages on a murdered girl's phone, advertisers withdrew their business. Rupert Murdoch, who owned the Sunday tabloid among a zillion other media holdings, shut the paper down.

DOLIGHAN, QMI Agency

McCULLOUGH

MOU, *Toronto Star*

DE ADDER

PASCAL, *The Gazette*, Montreal

GRASTON, *Windsor Star*

DE ADDER, *Metro*

Last stop on the
royal visit: Calgary.

"That's enough.
We're going home."

CHAPLEAU, *La Presse*, Montreal

PERRY

CUMMINGS, *Winnipeg Free Press*

PERRY

Canadian troops headed home, formally ending five years of combat and counterinsurgency in Kandahar province in Afghanistan. However, close to a thousand Canadian soldiers were to remain in Afghanistan until 2014 to train Afghan soldiers. Democrat Barack Obama and a U.S. House of Representatives steered by Tea Party Republicans played a game of chicken, managing just in time to raise the government's debt ceiling. One agency nevertheless lowered the U.S. debt rating. NDP Leader Jack Layton, having battled prostate cancer, learned that he had a new cancer to fight and took a leave of absence. He died on Aug. 22, and was given a state funeral.

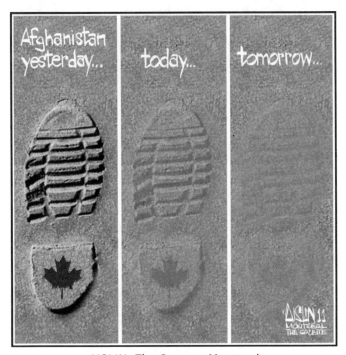

AISLIN, *The Gazette*, Montreal

BADO, *Le Droit*, Ottawa

RAESIDE, *Times Colonist*, Victoria

CUMMINGS, *Winnipeg Free Press*

CUMMINGS, *Winnipeg Free Press*

GABLE, *The Globe and Mail*

ROSEN, *The Montreal Mirror*

CORRIGAN, *Toronto Star*

MURPHY, *The Province*, Vancouver

BIOGRAPHIES

AISLIN is the name of TERRY MOSHER's eldest daughter and the nom de plume he has used as the editorial-page cartoonist for *The Gazette* in Montreal since 1972. Mosher has produced numerous collections of his own cartoons or books that he has illustrated; his 42nd book, *Aislin's Shenanigans*, was published in the fall of 2009. He and journalist Peter Desbarats wrote *The Hecklers*, a history of political cartooning in Canada that was published in 1980. The recipient of many awards, in 2003 Mosher was appointed an Officer of the Order of Canada. In 2007, he received a Doctorate of Letters from McGill University – not bad, given that he's a terrible speller.

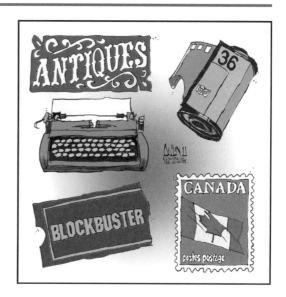

aislin@thegazette.canwest.com
www.aislin.com
http://cagle.com/politicalcartoons/PCcartoons/aislin.asp

GRAHAME ARNOULD was born in Manhattan in 1958, and some 19 years later studied economics at Queen's University in Kingston. Upon graduation he decided to become a cartoonist. On the strength of this work, he entered the world of advertising, where almost all his best work involved cartoons. His ad work won awards in Canada, the United States, Austria and Germany. He lives in Vancouver, where he contributes weekly editorial cartoons to *The Georgia Straight*. His gag and editorial cartoons are also distributed through *The New York Times* and his illustrations are distributed through Images.com in New York. The cartoon accompanying this biography won third prize at the 16th International Cartoon Exhibition in Zagreb, Croatia, in May 2011. The theme was vice.

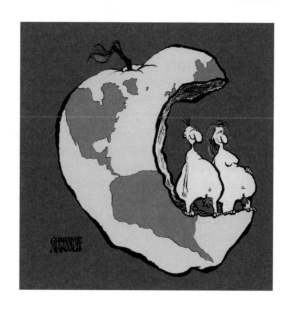

g_arnould@straight.com

BADO is GUY BADEAUX's last name pronounced phonetically. Born in Montreal in 1949, he worked there for ten years before moving to Ottawa in 1981 to become the editorial-page cartoonist for *Le Droit*. Author of nine collections of his own work and winner of the 1991 National Newspaper Award for Editorial Cartooning, he serves as treasurer of the Association of Canadian Editorial Cartoonists and was the previous editor of Portfoolio. His latest collection is *Sans dessins du Prophète*, Éditions David, Ottawa, 2011.

bado@ledroit.com
http://bado-badosblog.blogspot.com/
Twitter: @guybadeaux

BORIS is the nom de guerre of JACQUES GOLDSTYN. Born in Saint-Eugène d'Argentenay, Quebec, he graduated in 1980 from the University of Montreal with a degree in geology. After wasting his time in the oil industry in Calgary, he found his true love in Montreal: drawing. He co-founded *Les Débrouillards*, a celebrated children's scientific magazine for which he still illustrates articles and comic strips thirty years on. He has also collaborated with *Croc*, *Webdo Info*, *Relations*, *4 Temps*, *Le Couac* and *L'Aut'journal*. In 2000, he received the Michael Smith Award for Science Promotion and won two Grand Prix du Journalisme Indépendant (2009 and 2011). He is still an avid collector of rocks and fossils.

Born in Montreal in 1945, **SERGE CHAPLEAU** studied at l'École des Beaux-Arts and became a celebrity in Quebec in 1972 with a weekly full-colour caricature for *Perspectives*. He then created a puppet show, *La minute et quart à Gérard D*, for Radio-Québec. Returning to editorial cartooning on a daily basis at *Le Devoir* in the mid-eighties, he has been at *La Presse* since April 1996 and is a five-time winner of the National Newspaper Award. His half-hour animated series, *Et Dieu créa Laflaque*, is a staple of Radio-Canada on Sunday nights.

http://www.cyberpresse.ca/opinions/

"Don't miss this, coming soon on WikiLeaks: all the children's letters to Santa."

GARY CLEMENT is the editorial cartoonist for the *National Post*, a position he has held since last century. His freelance work has appeared in magazines and newspapers as diverse as *Mother Jones*, *The Wall Street Journal*, *The New York Times*, *Time* and *The Guardian*, and has been featured often in *American Illustration*. In 2007, one of his cartoons was a top 10 selection by *Time*, and his work has frequently appeared in *The Sunday New York Times* Week in Review section. He has written numerous children's books in Canada and the United States, and has written and illustrated two children's books: *Just Stay Put*, which was nominated for a Governor General's award for illustration in 1996, and *The Great Poochini*, which won the award in 1999. He continues to paint, draw and exhibit his own work in Toronto and Montreal.

Born in Toronto in 1951, **PATRICK CORRIGAN** studied fine arts at the Ontario College of Art before freelancing for *The Financial Post*, *Maclean's* and the *Toronto Star*. He joined the *Star* in 1983 as a full-time illustrator and has been drawing on the editorial page since 1995. Four times nominated for a National Newspaper Award, he has won several awards in illustration and graphics (Society of Newspaper Design, New York Art Directors Club, Advertising Design Club of Canada, Toronto Art Directors Club).

corrigan@thestar.ca
www.corrigan.ca
www.thestar.com
http://cagle.com/politicalcartoons/PCcartoons/corrigan.asp

ANDRÉ-PHILIPPE CÔTÉ, born in 1955, has been the editorial cartoonist of *Le Soleil* in Quebec City since the summer of 1997. Author of the comic strip *Baptiste*, he published six collections as well as thirty brief animated shorts of his character. He now draws the adventures of *le docteur Smog* for French publisher Casterman; two collections have come out so far. He also publishes an annual compendium of his best editorial work, *De tous les Côté*, and was twice finalist for the National Newspaper Award. His cartoons are frequently reprinted in *Courrier international* and *Le Monde*.

apcote@lesoleil.com

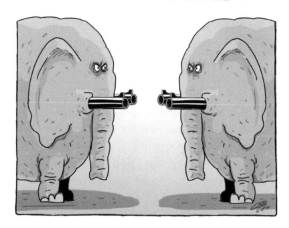

TENSION EXTRÊME EN CÔTE D'IVOIRE

Born in 1947 in St. Thomas, Ont., **DALE CUMMINGS** studied animation and illustration at Sheridan College in Oakville. During a brief stay in New York, he did some cartoons for *The New York Times*. He returned to Toronto in 1976, where he freelanced for *Last Post*, *Canadian Forum*, *Maclean's*, *Toronto Star*, *Canadian Magazine* and *This Magazine*. Full-time editorial cartoonist with the *Winnipeg Free Press* since 1981, he won the National Newspaper Award in 1983 and was a finalist in 2004.

http://zone.artizans.com/browse.htm?artist=7

MICHAEL DE ADDER is the editorial cartoonist for *The Times & Transcript* in Moncton and *The Daily Gleaner* in Fredericton. Born in Moncton, he studied painting, drawing and drinking at Mount Allison University, receiving a Bachelor of Fine Arts in 1991. His work also appears regularly in the *Parliament Hill Times* and *Metro Canada*, and is syndicated across North America through Artizans.com. He animates a weekly cartoon for CBC Nova Scotia. He's the first Canadian to win the American Association of Editorial Cartoonists' Golden Spike Award for the best cartoon killed by an editor. He won an Atlantic Journalism Innovation award in 2009 for television animation journalism, was short-listed for a National Newspaper Award in 2002 and has won three Atlantic Journalism Awards for Editorial Cartooning.

www.deadder.net

SUSAN DEWAR was born in Montreal in 1949. After attending Western University and the Toronto Teachers' College, she taught school for one year at Round Lake Reserve in the far north and three years in Toronto. In 1984, she became the editorial cartoonist for *The Calgary Sun*. In 1988, and five months pregnant, she returned to Ontario to become the cartoonist for the fledging *Ottawa Sun*. After 13 years in Ottawa, she moved to Toronto, where she shares duties at the Sun Media chain with Andy Donato and Tim Dolighan. Sue has won the National Business Writing Award and twelve Dunlop Awards, and has been nominated for the National Newspaper Award.

sue.dewar@sunmedia.ca
www.ottawasun.com/comment
http://zone.artizans.com/browse.htm?artist=99

DEWAR

TIM DOLIGHAN lives in Oshawa, Ont., with his wife Mary and children Caili, Shanna and John. After receiving degrees from Laurier, York and St. Paul U (none of which had anything to do with art), he started freelancing and illustrating for community newspapers in 1992. Tim currently provides daily editorial cartoons for Sun Media and sports cartoons for Sun Media's fanfare page. His work has received several national and Ontario community newspaper awards.

tim@dolighan.com
www.dolighan.com

DOLIGHAN.

ANDY DONATO was born in Scarborough in 1937. He graduated from Danforth Technical School in 1955 and worked in Eaton's as a layout artist. He joined *The Toronto Telegram* in 1961 as a graphic artist working in the promotion department. In 1968, he was appointed art director and began cartooning part-time. After the demise of the *Telegram*, he joined the *Toronto Sun*, and in 1974 began cartooning full-time. He took early retirement in 1997 and signed on as a freelancer. In 1985–86, he served as president of the Association of American Editorial Cartoonists.

www.torontosun.com/comment/cartoons

DUSAN PETRICIC (**DUSAN**) was born in Belgrade, Yugoslavia, in 1946. He graduated from the University of Belgrade's Faculty of Applied Arts and Design in 1969. His political cartoons and illustrations have regularly appeared in *The New York Times*, *The Wall Street Journal*, the *Toronto Star*, *Scientific American* and many other publications. As co-author and/or illustrator he has created more than 30 books for children, and is a recipient of many prestigious international awards. His most recent book is *My Toronto*, a collection of his cartoons and illustrations about the city. He was a professor of illustration and animation at the University of Belgrade, as well as at Sheridan College in Oakville, Ont. He has lived in Toronto since 1993 with his wife Dragana and daughter Mihaila.

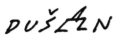

CHRISTIAN DAIGLE (**FLEG**) was born in Lévis, Quebec in 1963. A freelance graphic artist, illustrator and sculptor, he has been a cartoonist for *Yahoo Quebec* since April 14, 2010, and has contributed to *Le Soleil* in Quebec City since May 2002. He received the J.W. Bengough award in 1979 and the Albéric Bourgeois Prize in 1980.

info@fleg.net
www.fleg.net

Born in 1949 in Saskatoon, **BRIAN GABLE** studied fine arts at the University of Saskatchewan. Graduating with a B.Ed. from the University of Toronto in 1971, he taught art in Brockville and began freelancing for the *Brockville Recorder and Times* in 1977. In 1980 he started full-time with the *Regina Leader-Post* and is currently the editorial cartoonist for *The Globe and Mail*. He is a six-time winner of the National Newspaper Award for Editorial Cartooning.

bgable@globeandmail.ca
www.globeandmail.ca

Born in Montreal in 1951, and after studies having nothing to do with drawing, MICHEL GARNEAU (**GARNOTTE**) has contributed to many newspapers and magazines in Montreal, including *CROC*, *TV Hebdo*, *Protégez-vous*, *Titanic* (of which he was editor-in-chief), *Les Expos*, *Je me petit-débrouille*, *La Terre de chez nous* and *Nouvelles CSN*. He became the editorial cartoonist for *Le Devoir* in April 1996.

GARNOTTE

Berlusconi pursued by Justice.

MIKE GRASTON was born and raised in Montreal. He has been editorial cartoonist with *The Windsor Star* since 1980, after obtaining an honours degree in history from the University of Western Ontario and freelancing for *The Ottawa Citizen*. His work has appeared in most Canadian newspapers and a number of American publications, and has been featured on ABC's Nightline, CBC, CTV and CBC Newsworld. Through the combined efforts of the Art Gallery of Windsor and the National Archives of Canada, a 20-year retrospective of his work was exhibited in 2003. Married to Gina, he has three daughters: Lisa, Carly and Raquel.

www.grastoon.com
www.windsorstar.com/opinion/editorial-cartoons
http://cagle.com/politicalcartoons/PCcartoons/graston.asp

Born in Liverpool, England, **GRAHAM HARROP** emigrated to Canada at the age of seven, much to the relief of his family who stayed behind. His first cartoons appeared in the *Powell River News*, hastily drawn in the margins shortly after delivery. He now draws editorial cartoons for *The Vancouver Sun*, the comic panel *Back Bench* for *The Globe and Mail*, and the comic strip *Ten Cats* on Comics Sherpa.

ANTHONY JENKINS was born and raised in Toronto, where he delivered *The Globe and Mail* as a boy. He joined *The Globe* full-time after graduation from the University of Waterloo and a summer at the *Toronto Star*. In the 1980s, he took three long leaves of absence to travel on all the continents but Antarctica, sketching and producing the book *Traveler's Tales* for Lonely Planet. He began writing occasionally for *The Globe* around this time and continues to do so. He still travels widely, paints in acrylics for fun and profit, and lives in Toronto with two well-travelled and oft-painted daughters.

www.jenkinsdraws.com
ajenkins@globeandmail.ca

After 29 years of doodling political cartoons for *The Province* in Vancouver, **BOB KRIEGER** has been punted to the Sports section. When not trying to pawn himself off as knowing anything at all about hockey, the Vancouver native likes to cook, eat, drink, play a little guitar and start rumours regarding the impending comebacks of Bill Vander Zalm, Glen Clark and, now, Barry Bonds – essentially anything to get out of doing yard work. At the time of publication he has never been convicted of anything.

Born in 1950 in Swift Current, Sask., **JOHN LARTER** started at *The Lethbridge Herald* in 1974 and went to *The Edmonton Sun* in 1978. He was the *Toronto Star*'s editorial cartoonist from 1980 until his return west in 1989 to take the same position at *The Calgary Sun*. After being fired from the paper in 2001, John has gone on to more lucrative endeavours like.... delivering flyers and bottle collecting.

larterstudios@shaw.ca
http://zone.artizans.com/browse.htm?artist=9

GARETH LIND disproves the adage that environmentalists have no sense of humour with his comic strip *Footprint in Mouth*, which appears in Canada's environmental journal *Alternatives*. His weekly comic strip, *Weltschmerz*, satirized politics and contemporary life in Ontario weeklies from 1995 to 2007. That strip's characters reappeared on the Web for a year in *This Bright Future*. All his work is online at lindtoons.com. Lind is currently grappling with the demise of paying outlets for weekly (and, indeed, daily) cartoons. He runs his own graphic design firm in Guelph, Ont., where he lives with his wife and daughter.

Born in Hamilton in 1968, **GRAEME MACKAY** is *The Hamilton Spectator*'s resident editorial cartoonist. After studying politics and history at the University of Ottawa, he travelled Europe with pen and sketchbook in hand. In 1997, he began his professional career at *The Hamilton Spectator*. His cartoons have appeared in newspapers across Canada and the United States and in such magazines as *Maclean's*. Graeme and his wife Wendi live in Hamilton with their daughters Gillian and Jacqueline.

gmackay@thespec.com
http://www.mackaycartoons.net
http://zone.artizans.com/browse.htm?artist=76
http://cagle.com/politicalcartoons/PCcartoons/mackay.asp

BRUCE MacKINNON grew up in Antigonish, N.S., studied fine arts at Mount Allison University, and was a member of the graphic design program at the Nova Scotia College of Art and Design. He started doing a weekly editorial cartoon with *The Halifax Herald* in 1985 and began working full-time in August 1986. He has won numerous Atlantic Journalism Awards for editorial cartooning, was named "journalist of the year" in 1991, was the National Newspaper Award winner for both 1992 and 1993, and won second prize in the 2005 World Press Cartoon competition in Portugal. In 1996 he was awarded an honorary doctorate by St. Mary's University for his work in the field of editorial cartooning. His fourth book, *Penetration*, was released in September 2010 and is available from Nimbus Publishing.

mackinnonb@herald.ca
http://www.herald.ca
http://zone.artizans.com/browse.htm?artist=2

MALCOLM MAYES was born in 1962 in Edmonton. Editorial cartoonist for *The Edmonton Journal* since June 1986, he has seen his work appear in most major Canadian newspapers and many major American newspapers. His work has been featured in *Best Editorial Cartoons of the Year* (USA), *Reader's Digest* and *Maclean's*. His cartoons have been broadcast on the CBC, CNN, and Al Jazeera networks. He is also a principal of and contributor to Artizans.com, a global online distributor of cartoons, caricatures and illustrations.

mmayes@artizans.com
http://zone.artizans.com/browse.htm?artist=1

MONSTER TRUCK MASH.

J.J. McCULLOUGH was born in Vancouver in 1984. A graduate of Simon Fraser University, he spent much of his college life in the student journalism scene, writing and drawing for various student newspapers, including a brief period when he edited two different schools' papers simultaneously. J.J.'s cartoons have appeared in a variety of publications. He is the former editorial cartoonist of the *Western Standard* and the Port Coquitlam *Tri-City News*.

www.filibustercartoons.com

THEO MOUDAKIS (**MOU**) was born in 1965 in Montreal, where he began his career freelancing for *The Gazette* in 1986. In 1991 he started full-time with *The Halifax Daily News*, and in September 2000 he became editorial cartoonist for the *Toronto Star*. His work has appeared in most Canadian dailies and in *The New York Times*, *Time* and *Mad* magazine. He won the National Newspaper Award for editorial cartooning in 2004.

mou@thestar.ca
www.thestar.com
http://cagle.com/politicalcartoons/PCcartoons/Moudakis.asp

DAN MURPHY is a cartoonist for *The Province* in Vancouver. His animations for the paper's website can be found at: www.theprovince.com/opinion/murphy/index.html.

JOSE NEVES (**NEMO**) is a graduate of Université du Québec à Montréal, where he completed a masters degree in arts and communication. He also studied in France, where he did illustrations and character design for role-playing games. His cartoons have been published every week since 2005 in *The West End Times*, and he has freelanced for the *Sherbrooke Record* and *The Gazette*.

nemo.pix@gmail.com

GEOFF OLSON'S work has appeared in *The Globe and Mail*, *The Vancouver Sun*, the *National Post*, *Adbusters* and *This Magazine*. He is a regular cartoonist and writer for the magazine *Common Ground* and *The Vancouver Courier*, and has supplied commentary on both CBC Radio and CBC NewsWorld. His article series *The Deadly Spins* has been used in the course content of several U.S. and Canadian colleges, and his essay on malls appears in the fourth Canadian edition of the McGraw-Hill textbook *Sociology*.

www.geoffolson.com

DAVID PARKINS was born in 1955 in the U.K. and lived most of his life there. In 2006 he moved with his wife, Angie, and daughter, Hattie, to Ontario, where they have lived ever since. He draws a regular cartoon strip, written by the excellent Jason Sherman, for *The Walrus*, as well as a weekly cartoon for the British Columbia section of *The Globe and Mail*. Outside Canada, David is still a frequent contributor to *The Guardian* and creates a weekly cartoon for *The Times Educational Supplement*. His work often appears in *Nature*, and he illustrates children's books for publishers in Canada and abroad.

PASCAL ÉLIE'S cartoons appear in *The Gazette* in Montreal. He is also the regular cartoonist for several Montreal-area weeklies and contributes to *Law Times* and other publications in Quebec and English Canada. He has been freelancing for a couple of decades, but left his day job (as a legal editor) to become a full-time cartoonist in January 1998.

http://pascaltoons.com

GREG PERRY'S doodles appear daily in the *Telegraph-Journal* in New Brunswick, as well as in other newspapers across Canada. When he's not sharpening his crayons, Perry spends his time avoiding politicians.

Editorial cartoonist for the Victoria *Times Colonist* for 33 years, **ADRIAN RAESIDE** has seen his editorial cartoons appear in hundreds of publications worldwide. His comic strip *The Other Coast* appears in more than 350 newspapers.

INGRID RICE got her start cartooning in 1992, freelancing for *The Vancouver Sun*. She began self-syndicating in 1994 and is now published across Canada and throughout British Columbia. Although she has not won any major awards, she has appeared before the B.C. Press Council and been found to be reprehensible. Alongside cartooning, she is also a successful graphic designer and illustrator. In her spare time she is an authority on the health and psychology of guinea pigs, which has established her as an incredibly dull dinner guest.

ouridea@shaw.ca
http://cagle.com/politicalcartoons/PCcartoons/rice.asp

DAVE ROSEN is the editorial cartoonist for *The Montreal Mirror* and is syndicated by Artizans.com. Over the years, he has worked as a writer, stand-up comic and traffic reporter, and was once arrested for inciting a riot. He has published three books – *Megatoons*, *What Happened?!* and *The Quebec Neverendum Colouring & Activity Book* – none of which is likely to be made into a movie.

FRED SEBASTIAN'S work has appeared in publications and exhibitions throughout North America, including *Bon Appetit*, *Los Angeles Times Magazine*, *Canadian Living*, the *Toronto Star*, the *Ottawa Citizen* and *The New York Times Book Review*. In 1994, he won a Studio magazine merit award for Illustration and, in 2001, the National Press Club International Editorial Cartoon Competition on Press Freedom. He is a professor and co-ordinator at Algonquin College's School of Media and Design for the Professional Illustration program.

sebastian@magma.ca

Doubting Thomas

PHILIP STREET is a cartoonist and animator. He lives in Toronto with his wife, Vanessa Grant, and their son Jamie. His comic strip *Fisher* has appeared in *The Globe and Mail* since 1992, and a large chunk of it is perusable on his online archive at philipstreet.com.

WES TYRELL is a freelance illustrator and cartoonist born in Toronto in 1964 along with his twin brother. Prior to his life as a freelancer, he ran a hotel in Cuba and is writing about those bizarre experiences in a graphic novel entitled *Fidel & I.* Wes has drawn for *Maclean's*, *The Globe and Mail*, *Dogs in Canada* and the BBC. He is married and lives happily near the Scarborough Bluffs.

www.westyrell.com